THE HOLLYWOOD HISTORY OF WORLD WAR II

THE HOLLYWOOD HISTORY OF WORLD WAR II

ROBIN CROSS

St. Martin's Press
New York

First published in United States of America
in 1984 by St. Martin's Press Inc., 175 Fifth
Avenue, New York, NY 10010

© Copyright Charles Herridge Ltd 1984

Library of Congress # 84-50131
ISBN 0-312-38841-1

Produced by Charles Herridge Ltd
Woodacott, Northam, Bideford, Devon
Typeset by Lens Typesetting, Bideford,
Devon
Printed in Hong Kong by Leefung Asco
Printers

CONTENTS

JUMPIN' JACKBOOTS

Founded by a megalomaniac ex-Corporal short on inches and on humour, the Nazi party soon spread its tentacles into every aspect of German life except cookery. When destiny called Adolf Hitler and his unpleasant friends to power, their plans for world domination were ready, and so were their ornate uniforms.

Hurt in a hushed-up gay bar melée in Munich in 1923, Hitler receives emergency treatment from Rudolf Hess before facing a meeting of his supporters.

An exercise in naked power. Seated beneath a self portrait, unattractive Reichsmarschall Hermann Goering wonders whether to make an improper suggestion to a dissident journalist.

A rare picture of Josef Goebbels briefing the specially trained Reichstag fire-raising squad.

The Nuremberg Rallies were the showcase for the renascent Germany. In this previously unpublished photograph, members of the 12th Hamburg Stormtroopers salute the Führer as they march past the podium.

Small proto-Nazi Bubi Schwitters won prizes for book burning and art slashing.

BLITZKRIEG TO DUNKIRK

The diplomatic game of bluff and counter-bluff was over, umbrella diplomacy discredited. On the eve of war, Panzer divisons were poised to pour over the Polish border. The Blitzkrieg was about to be unleashed.

As tension mounts in Europe's capitals, crack German paratroops, in fitted 'chutes, train for behind-the-lines drops in Poland.

The moment of truth arrives. German armoured columns mass on the Polish border. In the foreground, the intrepid Colonel Otto Skorzeny, disguised as a civilian, crawls towards no man's land in a last-minute reconnaissance of the forward Polish positions.

Obsolete, ill-equipped and demoralized, the Polish army fell back before the German armoured thrusts. A last-ditch suicide squad bars the entrance to the Polish Corridor, grimly awaiting the final battle.

On 10 September 1939 the British Expeditionary Force arrives in France, well-equipped to deal with the winter ahead. Obliging locals show him the way to the Phoney War.

The Maginot Line falls, and the entire French high command is rounded up. The mighty bastion on France's Western border was still uncompleted when Field Marshal de Sade's command bunker was overrun by advance elements of the Hermann Goering Arctic Warfare division.

German pincer movements raced across the map of northern France, and British units found themselves cut off from retreat. Here British yeomanry are interrogated by a genial General 'Fast Heinz' Guderian in the wardroom of his battle tank.

As the British fell back, the indomitable spirit of the chirpy Tommy shone through in the face of imminent disaster and the unfamiliar hospitality of the typical French estaminet.

'The miracle of the small ships'. In good order and with a cry of 'Charge!' British units sprint for the boats at Dunkirk.

FRANCE LAYS DOWN HER ARMS

French generals lost face and faith when Hitler's men sidestepped their 'impregnable' Maginot Line and burst into France. As the iron-grey columns wound through the countryside, nothing could stem the jackbooted tide, etc., etc . . .

The Champs Elysées' fashionable bustle is stilled as the Mayor of Paris surrenders the city to officers of the Heinrich Himmler armoured euphonium division.

The hardships of Occupation. A humble French cottager is informed by a German billeting officer that she must find room for an entire SS division in her converted hayrick outside Orléans.

SPIES OF ALL NATIONS

Britain stood alone and America stood on the sidelines. Spy fever was rampant as the fifth column went about its insidious business.

Fiendishly subtle attempts to penetrate the innermost citadels of power. Disguised as Eleanor Roosevelt's younger sister, notorious Japanese agent Tootsie Tanaka lurks inconspicuously in the crush bar of The House of Representatives, her sensitive antennae picking up titbits of information falling from the tongues of unsuspecting politicians.

Opposite and above
When all else failed, there was nothing for it but to hide under the nearest available Important Desk and await developments.

A little-known episode in the relentless pyschological warfare campaign waged by the German Abwehr. Two top scientists examine a guinea pig to assess the initial results produced by their baldness-inducing beer. Plans to smuggle crates of the fiendish fluid into key British command centres were foiled when the U-boat carrying them ran aground on Brighton beach. At the end of the war OSS agents spirited the scientists away to America, where 30 years later they developed a defoliant lager for use in Vietnam.

FOKKERS OVER FOLKESTONE

In that glorious summer of 1940, the cloudless skies over southern England were darkened by the Luftwaffe. On the airfields below, the pilots of Fighter Command twiddled their thumbs and their handlebar moustaches, waited for their planes to arrive and gave each other silly nicknames.

Maintaining perfect formation, a flight of D Squadron's pre-war Rhinoceros fighter-bombers take off on their heroic interdictive raid on the Italian airship hangars at Knokke Le Zoult, 16 August, 1940.

16

Tempers run high in the Ops Room at Fighter Command HQ, Biggin Hill, over the controversial 'Big Wing' tactics advocated by Squadron Leader Enola Barrington-Skeffington (extreme left).

Debriefing shock. Pilot Officer Piers 'Binky' de Thruxton is reprimanded for engaging the enemy without wearing his Mae West or fastening his seat belt.

Opposite: Snarling their aggression, pilots of D Squadron, RAF Deep Twittering, race to their kites during a scramble at the height of 'Black Thursday' – 15 August 1940 – the day on which their airfield was subjected to heavy low-level bombing by Italian airships based on the Belgian coast.

Despite his DFC and two bars, 'Binky' suffered the ultimate penalty – providing the Home Guard Air Gun Division with a human target.

Top Battle of Britain ace Flying Officer Hugh
'Stuffy' Pemberton-Wally casts an
appreciative eye over the armoured gondola
of his personalized pursuit airship.

NAZI BUT NICE

Even the most dedicated SS man needed time for a spot of rest and relaxation. Despite the presence of a few dull sticks in their ranks, most of them were a fun-loving crew.

To relieve the mind-crushing boredom of a long weekend at Berchtesgaden, an SS officer readies himself to give some good-looking privates a playful thrashing.

In mellow after-dinner mood, a group of good-humoured SS pranksters suggest that their mess waiter be flayed alive. A good sport, he seems to be enjoying the joke.

A selfless act of charity. One of the many SS officers who in 1943 volunteered for a sponsored hanging to raise money for the Eastern Front. His colleagues give him some good-natured encouragement as they near their target.

Concern for the underprivileged is etched into the sensitive features of Oberleutnant Putzi von Slammer as he supervises the distribution of Red Cross parcels of pork and prawns in the Warsaw ghetto.

PEARL HARBOR, DAY OF INFAMY

On 1 December 1941, a Japanese carrier task force slipped its moorings and headed south – its mission to attack and destroy the vital Australian Fosters plant on Papua New Guinea. At the last moment its orders were changed. Swinging eastwards, it headed for the American naval base at Pearl Harbor. Was this the biggest Japanese blunder of the war?

As the Japanese battle fleet steams inexorably towards Pearl Harbor, officers relieve the tensions with a combat bonsai lecture.

Caught with his pants down, hapless Admiral Kimmel gropes for the Kummel as an aide informs him of the extent of destruction to the US Pacific Fleet.

General Hank Plugburger aims low to hit the leader of a Japanese landing party right between the eyes.

JAPAN SEEKS NEW MARKETS

In a matter of months the Japanese had rampaged all over South-East Asia in search of rubber. The Allies were ill-prepared for jungle warfare as the banzai brigades cut a savage swathe through Australian Arctic Warfare units, elements of the Royal Canadian Mounted Police and General MacArthur's Texas Rangers.

Bataan, the final hours. Armed to the teeth, General MacArthur's batman bids a sad farewell to two Marine Corps buddies as he prepares to accompany his general on the famous tactical withdrawal from the beleaguered fortress.

A Japanese officer forcibly requisitions an Australian diplomat's dripdry shirt in occupied Singapore.

A grim battle of willpower at a POW camp in the sweltering Burmese rain forest. Brutal commandant Major OK Banzai demonstates the superiority of Japanese wooden boxes over the inferior products of Western technology. After serving a 20-year sentence for war crimes, Banzai later became famous as the presenter of TV's Hara Kiri Cookery Course.

BRITAIN AT BAY

The British stood alone, but they refused to panic. Their greatest asset, complete national torpor, saw them through the dark days of 1940.

COLI-34.

The Home Guard is formed, but there is a desperate shortage of ammunition. Here a private in the 5th Loamshires is given a stern dressing down after firing his vital cap badge projectile at a low-flying Messerchmitt.

The Blitz reached its peak in the autumn of 1940. As German bombs rained down on the nation's capital, thousands of Londoners spent their nights sleeping on the platforms of the underground system.

A narrow miss at No 10 Downing Street. An unruffled Anthony Eden refuses to allow a Nazi blockbuster to interrupt a snatched game of snooker with Deputy Prime Minister Clement Atlee.

Fear of a fifth column reached epidemic proportions.

Rationing was introduced early in the war. Cheery Cockneys wait patiently outside a fishmongers in the old Kent Road for their weekly issue of whale steak.

MAKE MINE A TORPEDO

*In the grim months of 1943, the British and the Americans fought
a desperate battle to sweep the sea lanes free of the marauding
U-boat wolf packs of Admiral Karl 'Dunkin'' Doenitz.*

The last days of a surface raider. October 1939, and the German consul in Montevideo inspects the wrecked forward turret of the German pocket battleship *Graf Spee* as she lies at anchor, bottled up in the South American port by the Royal Navy.

A violent outbreak of botulism forces the hasty abandonment of the British submarine HMS *Scorcher* while on patrol in the Western Approaches.

An off-duty German rating enjoys a quiet jacuzzi aboard the massive long-range patrol submarine *Eva Braun.*

AMERICA ON THE MARCH

As the war gathered momentum, the full might of Uncle Sam's technological powerhouse ground into remorseless action.

Able Seaman Ignatz Prutz, inventor of the inflatable combat jockstrap, a vital life support system, demonstrates its release mechanism to an eager young US Navy divebomber pilot aboard the carrier *Codpiece*.

An instructress lends a hand as a wind machine goes berserk in the US Marines indoor parachute training school in Beverly Hills.

HANDS ACROSS THE SAND

Not since the days of Rudolph Valentino and the Sheikh had the desert seen so much action. In the battle for the strategically vital coastal winter break resorts, vast tank armies swept across the sea of sand, usually with no idea of where they were going.

Over a frugal breakfast in his mobile HQ, the 'Desert Fox', General Erwin Rommel, outlines his plans for the brilliant pincer movement at Sidi Rezegh, which caught the Cameron Highlanders with their kilts down.

Grim-faced Tommies wait for the balloon to go up in the underground car park of the Tobruk Hilton as Rommel's tanks advance.

Tunisia, 1943. As the defeated Axis armies fall back in disorder, a Canadian mobile barbecue unit provides vital logistical support to exhausted front-line troops.

German tank crews had to push their Panzers when their final assault on Montgomery's fixed defences ran out of gas.

FOR SOME THE WAR WAS OVER

With their eye on the postwar film industry, the British turned being a prisoner of war into a minor art form. Other ranks, unused to being away from home for long periods, were prone to crack up when Fritz cracked down. But for the officers it was just like being back at the old public school, with Gerry as the head prefect.

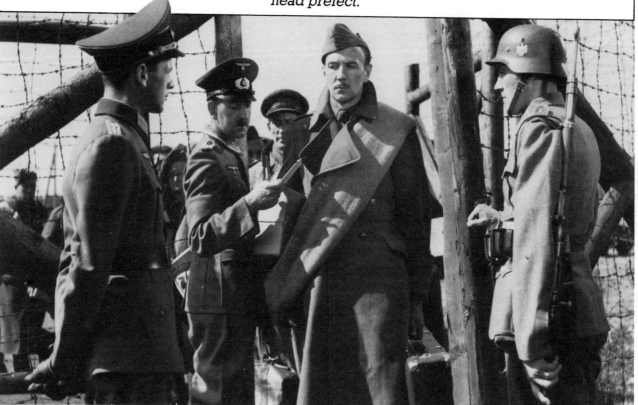

The sudden collapse of the French and British armies in June 1940 wrought havoc with POW camp reservations. A disappointed General Bertram Force-Feeding, who went into the bag at Dunkirk, is informed by the desk clerk at Stalag Luft XVII that the Hermann Goering honeymoon suite has already been taken by the French high command.

It seemed like a good idea at the time . . . British POWs at Stalag Luft XVII quickly lost interest in the morale boosting 'Bondage Week' suggested by officers of the Queen's Own Borderers.

Conditions in the camps were frequently grim. In the ballroom of the infamous mixed-sex camp Stalag Luft X, prisoners queue up to complain about the cooking.

Inmates of Stalag Luft X's Hut 22 draw cards to see who will wear the trousers.

GREAT ESCAPES NO 1

While a weather eye is kept open for patrolling German guards at Stalag Luft XVII, the latest consignment of escape instructors emerge from a bulky Red Cross parcel.

Three months later they masterminded the daring 'Operation Deep Ditch', tunnelling out of the camp under the unsuspecting noses of their German guards.

above
Next morning's roll call found the camp
empty but for these dummies.

below
The Gestapo listened for the tunnellers
on sophisticated sonar equipment, but
the birds had flown.

WINGS OVER GERMANY

Every night, on airfields all over Britain, heavily laden bombers taxied to take-off for just one more crack at the infamous ball-bearing plant at Schweinfurt.

632-123

In the early months of the war the RAF launched a massive bombing campaign against Germany, carpeting the Third Reich with a blizzard of double glazing and loft conversion leaflets. Aircrew of 'P for Pongo', a Mandrill fighter-bomber, admire their handiwork over Essen.

A less attractive target – even for the most experienced pilots – was the heavily defended Schweinfurt ball-bearing factory, but no amount of sulking could get you off the hook.

Strange things were likely to happen
to men who made one too many
Schweinfurt runs.

A WRAF artificer prepares to 'bomb up'
a flight of Wellingtons for the celebrated
'blockbuster' raid on the concrete U-
boat pens at Zeebrugge.

NOW IT CAN BE TOLD

Against the massive backdrop of total war, a million human dramas were played out. Here are just two of them.

The incredible tale of Captain Basil 'Bunty' Smallpiece, Churchill's personal agent, ace of spies and master of disguise.

left, infiltrating an Italian armoured column in North Africa disguised as the well-known General 'Electric Whiskers' Bergonzoli.

below, reporting to Stalin in his Kremlin bunker after a deep-penetration reconnaissance of German positions in the Urals.

left, going in with the US Marines in the first wave at D-Day. Long suspected of being 'the fifth man', Captain Smallpiece defected to the Soviet Union in 1956 and is now a full KGB Colonel in the Bolshoi Ballet.

For every hero there was a man who cracked. A casual flirtation over a pint of pink gin was the beginning of the end for much-decorated Wing Commander Jim 'Stuffy' Pogson. The lady in question was an Air Marshal's wife and Pogson was banished to the Arctic convoys, where a distressing misunderstanding in the Petty Officers' mess led to the final indignity: combat latrine duty in the Western Desert.

DATELINE MOSCOW

In June 1941 the steel claws of Hitler's elite Panzer divisions closed around Stalin's jugular as the German tank armies swept into Russia. The gloves were off, but the trouble was that the Germans didn't have any. Meanwhile it got colder and colder.

right: The rapid German advance was held up by the lack of adequate toilet facilities on the Pzkw Mk IV, mainstay of the armoured divisions. On the edge of the heavily defended Don Donetz Basin, a wary tank commander scans the horizon for signs of the enemy before relieving himself.

below right: As the merciless Russian winter closed in, German lack of preparedness was cruelly revealed. Most of their troops fought on in their summer combat clothing. Here infantrymen of von Rundstedt's mobile reserve keep warm with callisthenics before being thrown into action in the heavy fighting in the Kursk salient.

The men who fight and the women who must wait. A tearful farewell in a remote Georgian dacha as a Cossack takes leave of his wife.

Britain did what she could to help her gallant Russian allies. Stripped to the waist, heroic British Tommies get stuck into Finnish Arctic warfare units in savage fighting in the Karelian peninsula.

The hell that was Stalingrad. The Krasny Oktobar tractor factory witnessed grim hand-to-hand fighting as the struggle for the town reached a bloody climax.

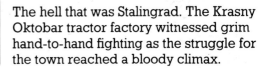

1943 and the tide turns on the Eastern Front. Stalin takes time off to demonstrate an outflanking movement to the wife of the British ambassador at a cocktail breakfast held in his Kremlin apartments.

THE SECRET WAR

Hundreds of miles behind the front lines, a stealthy but no less deadly war was waged by the backroom boys on both sides of the conflict.

In a top-secret installation US engineers gingerly defuse a pile of Mark IV Japanese incendiary dung.

In the remote Alaskan proving grounds, a team of scientists demonstrate their 8mm mastiff mortar.

Opposite: British matter transfer technology had reached such an advanced state of development by the spring of 1944 that the capability existed for clothing to be added en route. This enabled thousands of Australian troops to arrive in Britain fully equipped for the D-Day landings.

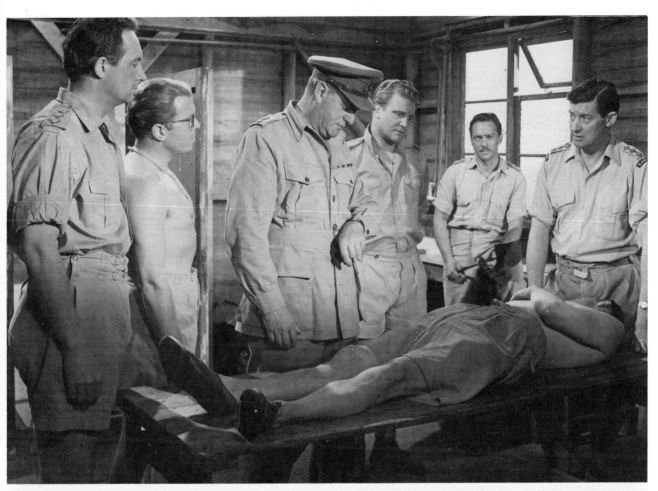

Allied Chiefs of Staff listen intently as boffin Barnes Wallis (with pipe) explains the workings of the human torpedo (seated).

As the war nears its end, an RAF technician readies Britain's first communications satellite for take-off.

The Big One. Scientists working on the hush-hush Manhattan Project set about assembling the first atomic bomb.

STEEL FISTS
IN IRON BOOTS

In Hitler's Festung Europa, from the Baltic to Brest, freedom-loving peoples groaned under the heel of the Nazi jackboot. It was good news for collaborationist cobblers, but the sheer tedium of it all drove many people into the Resistance.

A hard-of-hearing stalwart of the Maquis is surprised by an SS patrol as he listens for sounds of an approaching German armoured column, somewhere in France.

A *Signal* phographer is on hand for a photo-call during the quarter finals of the Quisling of the Year fashion show, Baden Baden, 1943.

Lower Bohemia, 1942. Party dignitaries wait for Reichsmarschall Hermann Goering to blow out the candles on his birthday cake.

Bored Nazi bigwigs settle down in their 3-D spectacles for a monster double feature at a late night drive-in in Vichy France.

A POCKETFUL OF BATTLESHIPS

While armies advanced and retreatful, while men sweated in steamy jungles, blistered in blazing deserts, and froze on the Eastern front, ships of all sizes and nearly all nations steamed relentlessly to and fro in various weather conditions.

The tragedy of the submarine USS *Silverfish,* which went down with heavy loss of life near Guadalcanal in August 1943. After the war, the facts were suppressed, but now they can be revealed. Captain Kurt Zipper's fatal mistake was in his choice of tapdancing veteran Lester 'Thunderboots' Conklin to close an impromptu concert in the wardroom. Zipper insisted on an encore and Conklin's no-holds-barred rendition of 'Putting On The Ritz' sent the *Silverfish* into a crash dive and split her hull from stem to stern. Then she shot to the surface, only to plunge back beneath the waves.

At the height of the Battle of Midway, damage control units of the US destroyer *Warren Gamaliel Harding* strive to keep their runaway macramé out of the hands of marauding Japanese crochet squads.

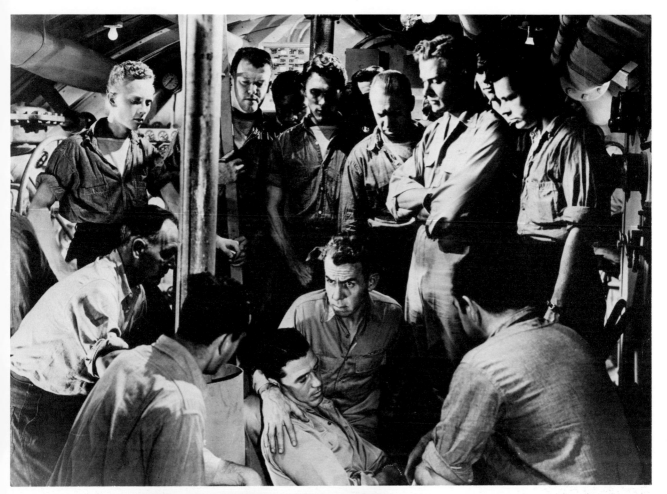

While the big guns boom overhead in the closing phase of the Battle of the Philippine Sea, anxious crewmen gather round as Captain Earl 'Crunch' Budweiser goes into labour. The result was the famous Budweiser quins.

May 27 1941, a crucial date in British naval history. In the bowels of the Royal Navy's operational headquarters, Rear Admiral Horace Hornblower (submerged) plots the closing stages of the campaign to sink the German pocket battleship *Bismarck*.

KAMIKAZES OVER KANBERRA

Scenes from the little-known foonote to the war, in which 85 Japanese divisions got lost in the outback.

Australian commando units receive a detailed briefing on the size of the enemy.

Opposite: A wary Australian naval engineer listens for signs of life inside a Japanese midget submarine stranded on a mud flat near Alice Springs.

Australian secret agents await their grim fate, a picnic at Hanging Rock, during the Japanese occupation of Queensland, summer 1942.

ITALY – THE SOFT UNDERBELLY

*With its vast reserves of uranium, rubber, olive oil and donkeys
Italy was a prize the Allies could not resist. In a combined
seaborne operation Allied troops overcame language barriers
and unfamiliar food as they thrust towards the Holy City.*

US military advisers and combat
construction workers (Hamburger Stand
Division) hit the beach at Anzio.

Battle-hardened Marine veterans – in the forefront of the bitter fighting which preceded the breakout from the beachhead – storm the Italian machine-gun nests ringing the American positions.

Resistance was stiffer than expected as Mussolini rushed his elite divisions south in an attempt to hurl the Allies back into the sea. Here, units of the tough Bersaglieri mountain regiment wait to be inspected by Il Duce before being hurled into the cauldron of war.

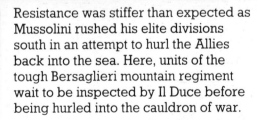

The Allied advance up the spine of Italy was slowed by the behind-the-lines activites of Mussolini's specially trained saboteurs, code-named 'Nubilioni'. In this picture the final drive on Monte Cassino comes to a grinding halt.

American ingenuity triumphs over adversity. Quartermaster Sergeant Dick van Nutter demonstrates a new mobile spaghetti dispenser to General Mark Clarke in the kitchen of his battle tank.

During a lull in the fighting for the last bastions of Field Marshal Kesselring's Gothic Line, men of the Seaforth Highlanders rehearse their Christmas production of 'Aida' under the eagle eye of their ENSA supervisor, the celebrated pantomime dame 'Winky' Warburton.

THE WAR LEADERS

Intimate portraits of the men on whose decisions the fate of nations hung in the balance.

December 1939 and Britain takes the offensive. Neville Chamberlain briefs the CO of 4 Commando on the plans for a lightning raid on the French coast. The attack finally went in on 2 August 1948.

Hitler used every device, including the enhanced acoustics of the bathtub, to mesmerize the population of Germany.

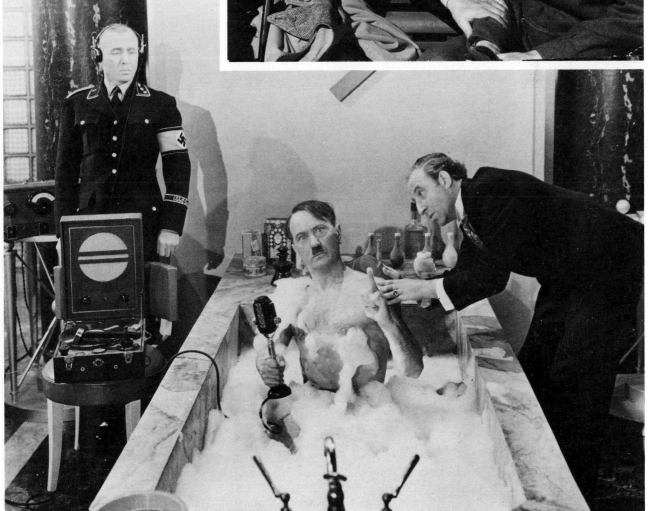

President Roosevelt deep in thought at the Yalta conference.

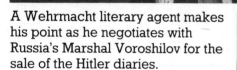

A Wehrmacht literary agent makes his point as he negotiates with Russia's Marshal Voroshilov for the sale of the Hitler diaries.

The moment of truth. General Eisenhower gives the go-ahead for Operation Overlord after a snatched meal at his South Coast headquarters.

ALLIED SAND IN HITLER'S FACE

After months of training and fighting in pubs, British, Commonwealth and U.S. troops swarmed on to Normandy's tranquil golden beaches, totally disrupting the Germans' four-year French holiday.

As Zero hour approaches, troops move up to their embarkation points through the dawn quiet of a sleeping English countryside.

Grim-faced and fully aware of their responsibilities, two men of 82nd Airborne Division psyche themselves up for their jump over Caen.

They swam all the way. Crack elements of General Patton's cross-Channel swimming battalion storm soggily up the beach somewhere in Normandy. Going in with the first wave was Major Esther Williams (extreme left with bazooka).

Louella Parsons is handed an iron rations issue by her faithful butler as the Press launch nears the Normandy coastline. Other war correspondents are, left to right, Walter Winchell, Walter Wanger, Walter Cronkite, Walter Hagen (sports section) and Walter Huston.

HELL IN THE PACIFIC

Bewitched, bothered and beleaguered on every side by small but tenacious Japs, America's finest battled bravely on until the tide began to turn. Hopping ferociously from one festering tropic isle to another they gradually beat back their mustard-coloured foe.

Wake Island, 8 December 1941, and US Marine projectionists keep the show rolling at their surrealist film festival while Japanese low-level bombers press home their attack.

As the struggle for Wake Island reaches its climax, a US Army disc jockey is forced at gunpoint to play a request for a Japanese commando clearly suffering from battle fatigue.

The early (1942) discovery that the invincible Banzai Boys could easily be made to cry gave US troops a decisive advantage in the Pacific campaign.

THE LONG ROAD BACK

Tempers flare at an NCOs' 'Excuse Me' during a lull in the fighting in the steamy jungles of Guadalcanal.

US Marines work up to combat readiness for the Iwo Jima landings aboard the assault ship USS *Turpentine.*

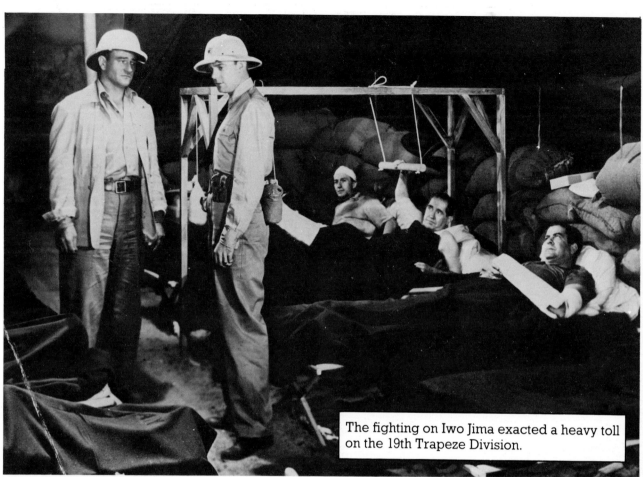

The fighting on Iwo Jima exacted a heavy toll on the 19th Trapeze Division.

The end nears. GIs round up the infamous Japanese Lon Dong water polo squad, who earlier in the war had vowed never to surrender.

THE BATTLE OF THE BULGE

Hitler's last desperate gamble to recapture the vital Christmas Tree plantations in the shell-torn Ardennes salient.

A British tank commander under heavy fire from German Panzers as he gives the order to steer his Belcher class main battle tank towards a dense formation of Tigers.

On the eve of Hitler's last big push, Field Marshal Fritz Sizzler is greeted by staff officers at his advanced battle headquarters on the edge of the snowbound Ardennes salient.

The beginning of the end. Troops of the US 3rd Army capture the entire command structure of the Martin Bormann naturist division at their last redoubt in a top-secret Bavarian schloss.

Bunkered. As Russian shells explode overhead in the blazing ruins of Berlin, the Führer bids farewell to Eva Braun before administering the final solution to himself. On the left (with moustache) is ace pilot Hanna Reitsch, waiting to fly out of the war-torn capital with Hitler's diaries, specially packed in hand-tooled matching luggage.

FILMOGRAPHY
and
ACKNOWLEDGMENTS

The stills in this definitive history have been taken from the following films. With apologies to Kenneth More, John Mills, Lassie, Erich von Stroheim, General 'Electric Whiskers' Bergonzoli and a cast of millions . . .

p7 (t) *The Hitler Gang*, Paramount, 1944
(b) *Pimpernel Smith*, British National, 1940
p8 (t) *The Strange Death of Adolf Hitler*,
Universal, 1943 (c) *Noah's Ark*, Warner, 1928
(b) *Tomorrow the World*, United Artists, 1944
p9 (t) *The Wooden Horse*, Rank, 1950
(b) *Secret Mission*, Fox, 1942
p10 (t) *Corregidor*, PRC, 1943 (c) *The Day
Will Dawn*, Rank, 1942 (b) *Bengal Brigade*,
Universal, 1954
p11 (t) *My Learned Friend*, Ealing, 1943
(c) *Johnny Frenchman*, Ealing, 1945 (b) *The
Commandos Strike at Dawn*, Columbia, 1942
p12 (t) *The Moon is Down*, Fox, 1943 (b) *Miss
V from Moscow*, PRC, 1942
p13 *Secret Agent of Japan*, Fox, 1942
p14 *The Black Parachute*, Columbia, 1943
p15 (t) *The Life and Death of Colonel Blimp*,
Rank, 1943 (b) *Confessions of a Nazi Spy*,
First National, 1939

p16 (t) *The First of the Few*, General Film
Distributors, 1942 (b) *Darkest Africa*,
Republic, 1936
p17 *Two-Man Submarine*, Columbia, 1944
(c) *Landfall*, ABPC, 1949 (b) *The Victors*,
Columbia, 1963
p18 *Above Us The Waves*, Rank, 1956
p19 *Hangmen Also Die*, United Artists, 1943
p20 *The Strange Death of Adolf Hitler*,
Universal, 1943 (c) *Pastor Hall*, Charter Films,
1940 (b) *Night of the Generals*, Columbia, 1966
p21 *Tora! Tora! Tora!*, Fox, 1970
p22 (t) *The More the Merrier*, Columbia,
1943 (b) *Cloak and Dagger*, Warner, 1946
p23 (t) *Halls of Montezuma*, Fox, 1950 (c) *An
American Guerrilla in the Philippines*, Fox,
1950 (b) *The Bridge on the River Kwai*,
Spiegel, 1957
p24 (t) *Get Cracking*, Columbia, 1943
(b) *Sodom and Gomorrah*, Titanus-Rank, 1963

p25 *Mrs Proudfood Shows a Light,* MoI, 1941 (c) *Little Tokyo USA,* Fox, 1942 (b) *For Whom the Bell Tolls,* Paramount, 1942
p26 (t) *Mrs Miniver,* MGM, 1942 (c) *The Sea Shall Not Have Them,* Rank, 1954 (b) *Western Approaches,* MoI, 1944
p27 (t) *Dive Bomber,* Warner, 1942 (b) *I Wanted Wings,* Paramount, 1942
p28 (t) *Five Graves to Cairo,* Paramount, 1943 (b) *Nine Men,* Ealing, 1943
p29 (t) *The Immortal Sergeant,* Fox, 1942 (b) *Tobruk,* Universal, 1972
p30 (t and b) *The Captive Heart,* Ealing, 1945
p31 (t) *Millions Like Us,* Rank, 1944 (b) *Albert RN,* Eros, 1953
p32 (t) *The Wooden Horse,* Rank, 1950 (b) *Edge of Darkness,* Warner, 1943
p33 (t) *Albert RN,* Eros, 1953 (b) *Submarine Alert,* Paramount, 1942
p34 (t) *God Is My Co-Pilot,* Warner, 1945 (b) *Twelve O' Clock High,* Fox, 1949
p35 (t) *The War Lover,* Columbia, 1962 (b) Paramount starlet Evelyn Venables, 1934
p36 *Saboteur,* Universal, 1942 (c) *Wings Over The Pacific,* Monogram, 1943 (b) *Courage of Lassie,* MGM, 1942
p37 (t) *Angels One Five,* Templar-ABP, 1954 (c) *The Cruel Sea,* Ealing, 1956 (b) *Ice Cold in Alex,* ABPC, 1958
p38 (t) *Battle of the Bulge,* Warner, 1965 (c) *Winged Victory,* Fox, 1944 (b) *Drums in the Night,* 1934
p39 (t) *Nine Men,* Ealing, 1943 (c) *The Dough-girls,* Warner, 1944 (b) *Blood on the Sun,* William Cagney, 1945
p40 (t) *The Naked and the Dead,* RKO, 1958 (b) *Back to God's Country,* Universal, 1953
p41 (t) *Danger Within,* British Lion, 1958 (b) *The Man Who Never Was,* Fox, 1955
p42 (t) *Albert RN,* Eros, 1953 (c) *Above Us the Waves,* Rank, 1956 (b) *See Here, Private Hargrove,* MGM, 1944
p43 (t) *Miss V from Moscow,* PRC, 1942 (b) *The Big Blockade,* Ealing, 1942

p44 (t) *Reunion in France,* MGM, 1942 (b) *The North Star,* Goldwyn, 1942
p45 *U-Boat Prisoner,* Columbia, 1944 (b) *Thunder Afloat,* MGM, 1939
p46 *PT 109,* Warner, 1963
p47 *Out of the Depths,* Columbia, 1945 (b) *Man Hunt,* Fox, 1941
p48 *The 49th Parallel,* MoI, 1942 (b) *Behind the Rising Sun,* RKO 1943
p49 *Adventures of Tartu,* MGM, 1942
p50 *Patton: Lust for Glory,* Fox, 1970
p51 (t) *How I Won the War,* United Artists, 1967 (c) *The Blue Dahlia,* Paramount, 1946
p52 (t) *Mister Roberts,* Warner, 1942 (b) *The Lost People,* Gainsborough, 1949
p53 (t) *The Life and Death of Colonel Blimp,* Rank, 1943 (b) *The Devil With Hitler,* Roach, 1943
p54 *The Demi-Paradise,* Two Cities, 1943 (c) *Escape,* MGM, 1940 (b) *The Masked Woman,* First National, 1925
p55 *Von Ryan's Express,* Fox, 1965
p56 (t) *Air Raid Wardens,* MGM, 1943 (c) *the Big Red One,* Lorimar, 1980 (b) *Lifeboat,* Fox, 1944
p57 (t and b) *Wake Island,* Paramount, 1942
p58 *Gung Ho!,* Universal, 1944
p59 (t) *Bataan,* MGM, 1943, (b) *Cry Havoc,* MGM, 1943
p60 (t) *Fighting Seabees,* Fox, 1944 (b) *The Naked and The Dead,* RKO, 1958
p61 *Convoy,* Ealing, 1940 (b) *I Cover the War,* Realart, 1937
p62 *The Devil's Brigade,* Wolper-United Artists (b) *Let George Do It,* Ealing, 1940

ACKNOWLEDGMENTS

11 (t,c), 12(b), 24 (b), 25(t), 28(b), 33(b), 43(t), 45(t), 53(b) British Film Institute. The remainder of the illustrations have been provided by the Kobal Collection.